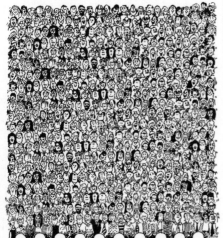

REACH
FOR THE BIG
TIME

REACH
FOR THE BIG
TIME

James Innes-Smith

BLOOMSBURY

First published in Great Britain in 2004

Copyright © 2004 by James Innes-Smith

The moral right of the author has been asserted

Bloomsbury Publishing Plc, 38 Soho Square,
London W1D 3HB

A CIP catalogue record for this book
is available from the British Library

ISBN 07475 7496 0

10 9 8 7 6 5 4 3 2 1

Printed in Hong Kong/China
by C&C Offset Printing Co.,Ltd.

All papers used by
Bloomsbury Publishing
are natural, recyclable
products made from wood
grown in well-managed forests.
The manufacturing processes
conform to the environmental
regulations of the country
of origin.

REACH
FOR THE BIG
TIME

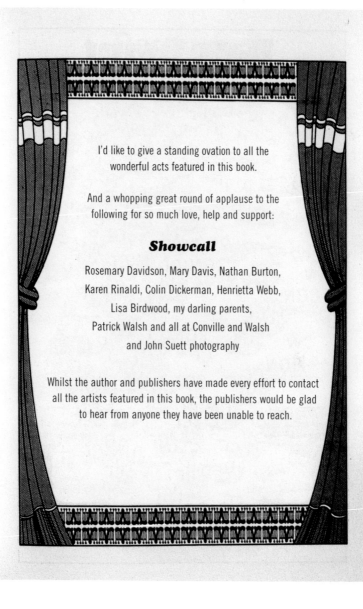

I'd like to give a standing ovation to all the
wonderful acts featured in this book.

And a whopping great round of applause to the
following for so much love, help and support:

Showcall

Rosemary Davidson, Mary Davis, Nathan Burton,
Karen Rinaldi, Colin Dickerman, Henrietta Webb,
Lisa Birdwood, my darling parents,
Patrick Walsh and all at Conville and Walsh
and John Suett photography

Be Amazed! Be Delighted!
Be Confounded!

Welcome to the world of light entertainment 70s style: a surreal place, full of double entendres, wacky spectacles, sticky-out teeth and loud check suits. Out of this strange and spangly land, a whole generation of all-round entertainers was born. Cuddly-named showmen like Brucie and Tarbie dominated Saturday night TV with their gentle brand of comedy song-and-dance routines. But Brucie and his golfing chums were only the tip of a very peculiar, glittery iceberg.

During the 70s and early 80s, when variety still topped the bill, hordes of eager young performers packed out seaside theatres across the land. These 'palaces of fun', usually perched precariously on the ends of rickety piers, were where the stars of TV-lite cut their comedy teeth. However, not everyone who performed there would be lucky enough to go on to become the next Doddy or Manning.

Although most of these hopefuls never made it to TV, there was still plenty of work to go around. In order to get noticed you needed to arm yourself with a snappy promotional flyer, something to let the snooty booking agents know you meant business. The format was simple: a decent photo, a description of the act itself and some colourfully chosen words describing how utterly amazed and astonishingly thrilled your audience will be. Throw in a couple of carefully edited local newspaper reviews and some glowing praise from random punters and watch those bookings roll in.

It's all a long way from the slick marketing and media savviness of today's young performers. Back then it was a long hard slog but once you were up and running, there were several possible routes you could take. Some artistes enjoyed the rough and tumble of the smoky northern club scene and corporate gig circuit, while others dreamed of Scandinavian cruise liners, holiday camps and hotel lobbies. An infinite world of weird opportunities was theirs for the taking and at the back of it all, the exciting possibility of one day making it big. The world of entertainment may have changed beyond recognition in the last twenty-five years but the light entertainers and variety artistes are still out there, plugging away and dreaming of one day reaching the **BIG TIME**.

Reach for the Big Time ...
Anything is possible

JULIEN

Organist / Pianist / Keyboard / Vocalist

JULIEN COOKE

INTRODUCING
"Reggie Mental"

Comedy entertainer "Reggie Mental" has brought a breath of fresh air
to the cabaret scene and can now offer this exciting new show.

A truly professional act of the highest calibre.

This show is traditional variety comedy at its best,
brought up to date with "Reggie Mental's" fast modern presentation.

"Reggie Mental" is one of Britain's finest young impressionists,
and his quick wit and timing makes him a unique stand up comedian.

This really is a superb cabaret suitable for all the family whether a hotel, restaurant
or holiday centre "Reggie Mental" will give you a night to remember.

4 Admiralty Road, Great Yarmouth, Norfolk NR30 3DG

MR GRAHAM BINMORE

. . . almost sophisticated

Agency:

Peter G Foot Entertainments

240 TOLWORTH RISE SOUTH
SURBITON SURREY

PAUL JAMES
"IS A VERY FUNNY MAN"

Personal Management:
Alex Jacks
Ajax Entertainments
52 Bounces Road
London N9 8HX

KEN JOY

VISUALIST

*

INSTRUMENTALIST

*

FUNNIEST

K.A.J. Productions
224 Hamlet Court Road, Westcliff-on-Sea, Essex.

LAUGHING
LARRY LARKIN

Slightly Insane

BRITAIN'S NEWEST COMEDIAN

Direct from TV's Oswaldtwistle Night Out

Quotes:
"I thought you were fantastic" — a man in a toilet in a working men's club.
"I thought you were very funny" — a woman in the street at Oswaldtwistle.

Sole representation in the U.K.:
Kim Holmes, Showbusiness Ent Agency,
113 Hickings Lane, Stapleford, Notts

IAN "SLUDGE" LEES

Runner up in the Club Mirror National Awards 1978 and 1979

Midlands Comedian of the Year 1979

Star of "New Faces" and "Tiswoz"

Jake Elcock
Astra International Entertainments
"Lafayette" Thornley Street, Wolverhampton

HOMER NOODLEMAN
INTERNATIONAL ENTERTAINER, TV & CABARET ARTISTE

T.V., Summer Shows, Panto, etc.
Principal Comedian: act ranges from zany & visual to stand-up patter & audience participation.

Theatre & Cabaret:
A Variety show on his own. Complete One-Man show up to 2 hours.
"MEET HOMER NOODLEMAN"
Comedian: Vocalist: Multi-instrumentalist (8 instruments)
Ventriloquist: Impressionist: Comedy-Magician.
Contact: **Homer Noodleman, 304, Cheetham Hill Road, Dukinfield, Cheshire**

or any leading agent.

ODD COUPLE

VOCAL — COMEDY — INSTRUMENTAL — DUO

C. M. Management
Charles McKay 17 Colewood Drive,
Strood,
Kent, England

Cascade Entertainment Agency
10 Avon St.
Hamilton,
Scotland

SHEER ELEGANCE

INTERNATIONAL RECORDING STARS OF
T.V., FIMS and CABARET

139 Bulverhythe Road, St Leonards on Sea, East Sussex TN38 8AF

Member C.E.A.C.   DoE Lic SE(B) 1426   VAEC 288

THE SWEET ILLUSION DANCE BAND

"The main aim of *'SWEET ILLUSION'* is versatility. It's a mixed band, musically speaking, that can create sounds from pop to middle-of-the-road, to the big band sound, all with a polish and a sheen that glows from their stage presentation.

"They never let up for a moment, and keep music alive for the entire time they are on stage."

JEFF MUDGE   CABARET & VARIETY REVUE

NO SOLE AGENT

12 STOWFORD ROAD
HEADINGTON
OXFORD OX3 9PJ

ROY BAKER

The Sensational Hypnotist

Touring Theatres and Clubs, Roy Baker has always caused a sensation, with people returning to see his fantastic Hypnotic Act again and again.

Quick return bookings and standing ovations are the order of the day when Roy is around.

He has made several T.V. appearances, has a superb Cabaret Act and with the flair of the complete showman does a fine one-man show.

His excellent promotion material backed up by a first class performance makes him the ideal choice for Civic Theatres and Summer Seasons.

This year he has toured the Pontin Holiday Camps for the full Summer Season filling the Startime Cabaret Spot and has been asked to return to do the Christmas Season for them.

Only first Class Offers considered.

NOT SOLELY REPRESENTED.
All enquiries to: — Roy Baker, 45, Salisbury Avenue,
Rainham, Gillingham, Kent, ME8 0BL

DISCO KID

THE SOUTH COAST INTERNATIONAL ROAD SHOW

NOT SO MUCH A *DISCO* AS A *HAPPENING*

Available for RESIDENCIES, RADIO, CLUBS & SPECIAL EVENTS

ENQUIRIES:

PETE:
    2 Nettlecombe   **OR**
    Shaftesbury
    Dorset

                                              Personal Management
                                  Ding's Disc Entertainments
                                       77 Hartington Street
                                                 Bedford

ALAN FOX

COMEDIAN and VOCALIST
STRONG PRODUCTION COMEDIAN

Appearances include:

*Granada Television, Summer Seasons. Last five years: Blackpool, Isle of Man, Jersey (5 times).
Most leading British cabaret dates.*

All enquiries:
3 Lavington Road, South Shields, Tyne & Wear NE34 6EY

AL NICHOLLS

Britain's Leading Comedy Speciality Act

Recent Television appearances include:
Opportunity Knocks, Be My Guest, What Fettle.

Offers invited for full weeks home or abroad, also
Top class Summer Season or Cruise.

Sole Representation
ROY MOZLEY ASSOCIATES LTD.
1st Floor Suite
St James Buildings
65a Oxford St
Manchester 1

DICK PLEASANT

COMEDIAN FOR ALL OCCASIONS

COMEDY ALL THE WAY

Several Television Appearances

Member of Equity   **No Sole Agent**
P.A: 47 Gratton Court, Staveley, Chesterfield, Derbyshire

Rotophone answering service if not immediately available

KENNY CANTOR

Sole Management:
FLOREAT PRODUCTIONS (Jimmy Grafton)
46 ST JAMES'S PLACE, SW1

Publicity Representatives: J. & J. Enterprises

BENNY PALMER

Comedian — Compere

Enquiries:
CONSTRUCTION HOUSE, HORNCHURCH, ESSEX

MALCOLM JAMES McVICAR

Male Vocalist

Surely one of the great voices of the decade. Past lead roles in "My Fair Lady", "Mame", "Fiddler on the Roof", Pantomime.
A busy Summer '74 in cabaret in Torbay, combining with a ten week show in Dartmouth. Then after returning from Portugal in October, Malcolm is available for pantomime and cabaret.

M & J PROMOTIONS, 100 SHERWELL VALLEY ROAD
CHELSTON, TORQUAY TQ2 6EX

Johnnie Bryan

BIG Laughs from beginning to end

"He reminds me of Mr. Pickwick"
—ATV's 'New Faces' panellist

TERRY BURGESS

and his

CAVALCADE OF FUN

Ideal Entertainment for the after-dinner show, club, cabaret, theatre show.
An act to suit all occasions. With audience participation.
Fast moving with laughs all the way. Comedy magic with the emphasis on the comedy.
Terry Burgess has an act you can sit back and enjoy. A very visual and colourful entertainment that can be performed anywhere, surrounded. An up-to-the-minute act that makes the audience roar with laughter. A brand of humour that is adapted to the audience. Musical accompaniment is not essential.
Terry Burgess has appeared in London's leading hotels including The Savoy, Grosvenor and Cafe Royal.
If you are wondering what kind of entertainment to provide at your next function liven things up with Terry Burgess and solve your problem.

All Enquiries to: TERRY BURGESS,
2 HILL CRESCENT, HARROW, MIDDLESEX

FRANK LEYTON

VOCALIST

TV Radio
First class offers home or abroad considered
Also available with own P.A. and own guitar accompaniment for
smaller clubs.

All enquiries to: WALLY DENT ENTERTAINMENTS,
121a WOODLANDS AVENUE, WEST BYFLEET, SURREY

ABBE LEYLAND

"This songbird supreme captivates her audiences in no uncertain manner" —
THE STAGE 1973

Audiences in the West End, cabaret and theatre venues throughout this country and abroad are under Abbe's spell from the moment she opens her act, commanding attention by projecting her instinctive and dynamic talent.

Stunningly attired, her solo performances are immaculately conceived and expertly executed.

Going from strength to strength this girl has a stunning future . . .

Enquiries:
12 Riverside Gardens, Henley-in-Arden, Warwickshire

CHARLIE LEA

"FROLICS TO YOU"

"Not only is Charlie Lea a very good compere, he has a great cabaret act of his own, and his big claim to fame in South Africa will be that he went through almost his entire act without a blue joke"

SOUTH AFRICA PRESS.

"Charlie Lea had the first night audience in the palm of his hand from his opening gags onwards"

JERSEY PRESS

"Charlie Lea radiates happiness, he is a comedian who can communicate"

LONDON EVENING NEWS.

"Charlie Lea is a very funny young man, he has great potential, and will be a star."
— KEN DODD

"Charlie Lea is a splendid 'Wishee Washee'; he never got the girl, but that didn't matter, he had the audience every one of them, they laughed at him and they loved him." —— PETERBOROUGH PRESS

10 VINCENT CLOSE
HAINAULT, ESSEX

TWICE AS NICE

VOCAL & INSTRUMENTAL HARMONY

For strict tempo and the latest pops
Ideal for backing cabaret and shows

BOBBY BENNETT

Sole Representation:
NORMAN MURRAY,
London Management Ltd.,
235-241 Regent Street,
London W1A 2JT

HOT FOOT GALE

Quote by CHRIS OAKLEY, Yorkshire Evening Post: "ONE OF THE BEST ROCK & ROLL GROUPS IN BRITAIN TODAY."

Their act includes all the excitement of the old-time rock shows — dancing on the piano, playing the keys with boot heels, drummers standing on drums — and Mick Gale brings a ROCKIN' TOUCH to the PIANO that many of the greats would be proud to own.

Highly rated wherever they appear.
SEVERAL TV SHOWS for Yorkshire TV producer NICK GREY.

Representation:

Philip Brooke Enterprises

43 Manchester Road, Greenfield, Oldham OL3 7ES

THE DENTONES

Summer Season:
Highly successful 16 weeks at
Winter Gardens Leisure Centre, Morecambe

This self-contained act can also provide backing for
Cabaret Artistes or play for dancing. Lead singer Frankie
doubles as compere.

Now accepting bookings for October onwards

Management: NORMAN THEWLIS

CANDY ROCK

THREE FANTASTIC LADS ...

This exciting, talented young trio is fast making a big, BIG name. With their own original songs and fabulous natural personalities, they've scored huge hits on C.S.E. tours — the University scene — and they're SPECIALLY POPULAR on the CLUB CIRCUIT.

YOU'VE GOT TO HEAR THEM TO BELIEVE IT!

Personal Management: EVE PORTWAY

Barry & Dinky

VOCAL DUO

Enquiries to:

Communications:
GARRY BROWN ASSOCS.,
(INTERNATIONAL) LTD.

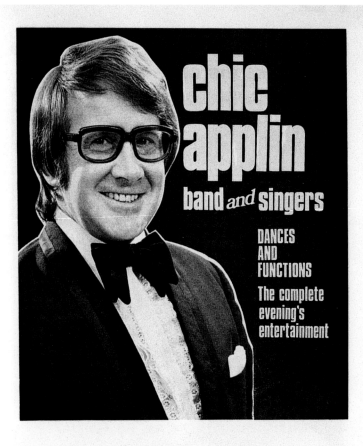

The
AMAZING MARGOES

"MIND-READING CAN BE FUN ! !"

This is a world-travelled act, with great experience in every branch of
show-business. It combines the exuberant personality of AL DAVIS
— a great showman, the charm of "MARGIE", fun, audience
participation, and "unfathomable" "mind-reading".
Suitable for ANY venue. Have appeared on Bailey circuit, "Tommy
Steele Spectacular", "New Faces" etc.

Contact AL DAVIS, Flat 5, Royston Court,
Carlton Road, Whalley Range, Manchester 16

THE AMAZING

KAT MANDU

INTERNATIONAL ARTISTE

THE WORLD'S MOST FAMOUS
Para - Stuntologist

Specialises in

- YOGA and ESCAPOLOGY
- HUMAN SUSPENSION
- WALKING on a LADDER of RAZOR-BLADES
- FIVE FOOT LEAP onto BROKEN GLASS
- HUMAN HANGING and STRANGULATION
- LYING on BROKEN GLASS with persons on his chest
- SMASHING BOTTLES across his BARE THROAT
- HEAD STAND on BROKEN GLASS
- and MANY OTHER AMAZING FEATS

The most BREATH-TAKING ACT in showbusiness today
His HAIR-RAISING FEATS will
THRILL and AMAZE EVERY AUDIENCE

BBC—ATV—Southern TV— Anglia TV— and RADIO

Personal Manager: PAUL H. BAKER
ARTISTE PROMOTIONS (BRIGHTON)
362 South Coast Road, Telscombe Cliffs, near Brighton, Sussex

TONY TADMAN
COMEDIAN — IMPRESSIONIST — COMPERE

There is no doubt that TONY TADMAN has the gift that all funny comedians possess;
a cheeky warmth and a raw brashness, without losing that quality and style which
has been acquired the hard way.

No stranger to the 'hard way', Tony is an ex-International Racing Cyclist, who
changed from turning fast wheels to fast impressions, and is proving a popular
support and compere for top names at home and abroad with his friendly image.

With today's undervalued use of the word 'Star', this likeable lad from the Lake
District reckons he just aims to be a busy comedian, but laughing audiences around
the Country are tipping Tony Tadman to be a top funny man of the future.

Enquiries:
Ronnie Stewart Entertainments
4 Ledwell Drive, Glenfield, Leicester

GAVIN PRIME
SENSATIONAL COMEDY ENTERTAINER

PHOTO:— AUG-81

The following press quotes were published not more than nine months before the copy deadline of this directory:—

"A whirlwind of song, dance and comedy" . . . *"Never a dull moment"*
FRED NORRIS, B.ham Evening Mail.

"He lives and breathes pure entertainment with an overwhelming expertise in creative ideas and the use of props" . . . *"Totally absorbs his audience".* BARRY BALMAYNE, **The Stage.**

"The Heir Apparent to Ken Dodd". . . PETER McGARRY; **Coventry Telegraph**

"He is something new, not a stand-up joke telling comedian" RAY SEATON, **Express and Star.**

RAPIDLY BUILDING A CULT FOLLOWING IN THE MIDLANDS
SOLO ACT OR GAVAMANIA COMEDY PACKAGE SHOW

BOB RITCHIE

COMEDIAN
"Unknown to Millions"
Available for Summer Season 1978
All good offers welcome

**Northern Star Management,
Suite 7, 13 Walker Terrace,
Gateshead, Tyne and Wear, NE8 1EB**

WILD WALT BROWN

Photo: Alan Studios

UNPROFESSIONAL RUBBISH EQUALLY CHAOTIC IN NIGHT CLUB MUSIC HALL OR DISCOTHEQUE.

WHY THIS ENIGMA OF THE ENTERTAINMENT WORLD CONTINUED TO PACK INLAND VENUES THROUGHOUT THAT LONG HOT SUMMER IS BEYOND COMPREHENSION.

IAIN ALLAN AGENCY
65 Cobden Hill,
Radlett, Herts.

Wild Walt Brown
53 Cranes Park,
Surbiton, Surrey.

TYKE

Superb vocal instrumental
& Comedy Group

Appearing in cabaret, clubs & colleges.
Currently on release "A Taste of Tyke" (Magnum Records)

A QUALITY ATTRACTION FOR QUALITY VENUES

Contact:
Roger Bloom
McLeod Holden Enterprises Ltd
PO Box 3, Hessle
North Humberside HU13 9LF

"ASTRA"

ILLUSION AND SPECIALITY

KEN BAINES & PEGGY

"VENTRILOQUIALLY UNIQUE"

Offers invited, cabaret, variety and O.T.M.H.

No sole agent

10 Hillcrest Road, Chaddesden, Derby

JACKIE CARLTON

Juvenile lead - The North's answer to Peter Wyngarde - Very versatile - Good with make-up for character work. Since 'NEW FACES' and 'THE LONDON PALLADIUM' I haven't stopped working - but would love to get back into Show Biz.

Forthcoming engagements Nov 24th week Manchester Palace in 'The Lancashire Laugh-in'. (Box office now open.) Dame Trot 'Red Riding Hood' New Century Theatre Manchester (3rd Year.) "Comedians we've got; genuine funny men are a rare find; Jackie Carlton is one such rarity"   *- Beryl Jones (Manchester Evening News).*
"Adds insult to comedy, with that added ingredient warmth - Jackie Carlton is the real thing. Beware of imitation"
                                                                    Radio Piccadilly.

No sole agent
Direct 10 Coulsden Drive, Blackley, Manchester 9.

Personal Manager Gordon Pleasant

JEAN (Granny) COPE

Has been acting Grannies, sad and funny, for forty years.
Still going strong. Has tricycle - will travel.

JEAN COPE

JOHNNY COX

COMEDIAN
No singing!!
No instruments!!
Hilarious comedy
all the way

making a big impact
throughout Clubland
and
tipped by many to reach
the very top

Available for:
TV shows, commercials
one nighters and
full week cabaret engagements

BOOK EARLY!
He's a busy man

All enquiries:
143 Westminster Crescent, Intake, Doncaster

CHARLIE DAZE

BRILLIANT COMIC

All enquiries to   Mr. George Forster,
Fairworld Agency,
Sombrero Club,
Front Street,
Chester-le-Street,

"TAKE OFF"

TAKES YOU

TAKE OFF

EVERYWHERE

LONDON'S LATEST FLOORSHOW

Enquiries to: Hilda Durante

CHRIS SMITH

A sophisticated combination of
Comedy Ventriloquism, Novel Puppets plus audience participation,
for television, cabaret, functions etc...

Enquiries:- Chalk Hill, 51 Alexandra Road, Reading.

IAN SANDS

Top Class Cabaret & Theatre Comedian
Presenting a refreshingly original style of humour

Recent venues played include:
Wakefield Theatre Club; Jollees, Stoke
New Cresta, Solihull; Villa Marina, Isle of Man.

Recent T.V. appearance YORKSHIRE T.V.'s "CALENDAR PEOPLE"

Representation:- **Barry McManus,
Action Enterprises,
The Textile Hall, Aldams Road,
Dewsbury, West Yorkshire,**

STEVE RIVERS
Guitar Vocalist

COUNTRY & WESTERN and FOLK

THEATRE, CLUB AND CABARET ENTERTAINER

All enquiries: 6 Flax Close, Hollywood, near Birmingham

The **biggest** laughs from the **smallest** act in show-business.

The Mini-Tones

JACK MAYES

The

LAUGH ALONG - SING ALONG

Comedy Act

...with a few balloons
to blow up the audience with laughs!

Bookings: QE2; Cafe Royal; Cesars Palace, Luton; Hilton; Clubs etc.

153 Derby Way, Stevenage SG1 5TN, Herts

THELMA JOYCE

BRILLIANT ELECTRONIC ORGANIST

Available for cabaret, dancing etc. All types of music played to suit everyone. Has own electronic organ and drummer available if required Has had great acclaim wherever asked to play. Will travel anywhere to please

Sole Representation NEIL CROSSLAND PROMOTIONS
15 Torksey Close, Manor Park Estate, Bessacarr, Doncaster,

GENTLE & GIANT

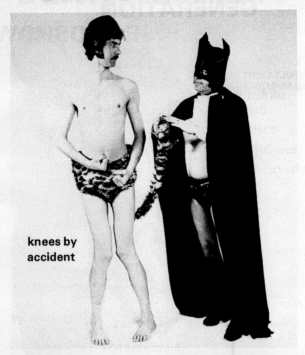

knees by
accident

BOOKERS AND MUSICAL KLEPTOMANIACS
TAKE NOTE
THAT
Gentle and Giant are available for Summer Season '76, also
Pantomime '76 and cabaret weeks at your convenience
Gentle and Giant - a new comedy double-act with strong visual appeal.
RECENT QUOTES:

After 10 mins I was ecstatic, I have never seen such a funny act - *Gentle*
I was with him at the time, and can vouch for his every word - *Giant* *(he owes me money)*

ANY OFFERS CONSIDERED, MONEY PREFERRED.
ENQUIRIES Ian England Management, 11 Toftingall Avenue, Birchgrove.

Carolina Blue
STYLISH KEYBOARDS AND VOCAL ENTERTAINMENT
(North West based)

Civil Weddings and Receptions a Speciality
Private Parties; Functions; Dancing

★ ★ ★

From Solo Piano to full Orchestral Music

Please ring Caroline for further information

DAVE ADAMS

NOT FOR THE FAINT HEARTED

Stag Specialist, also hen, after dinner, military and
unshockable mixed audiences.

North East Contact:
RGA PROMOTIONS

International Contact
JB PROMOTIONS

VINCE EAGER

A Tower of Entertainment

A dynamic all round vocal and comedy entertainer.
International Television, radio and recording star.
Cabaret, Productions shows, Pantos, etc.

Contact Personal Manager: TREVOR GEORGE (ATPM)
42 MARLDON ROAD, SHIPHAY, TORQUAY, DEVON

RAY McVAY
and his Orchestra

Winners of the "CARL-ALAN AWARD" for 1972

for the Most Popular Orchestra.

MECCA AGENCY INTERNATIONAL LTD
22, SHAFTESBURY AVENUE, LONDON, W1V 8AP

THE SHADES OF HARMONY

"THE SHADES OF HARMONY" are gifted — varied with expression with a facility and correctness which attests their great sensibility. When listening to these two young artists, one recalls the magic of Nina and Fredrick, others that come to mind are Miki and Griff, but they have their own originality in the presentation of their act."

The Press said of them, "Their fine performance left me in no doubt that we are going to hear a lot more of this very Talented Duo."

To make your cabaret complete, why not book The Shades of Harmony?

Cabaret, Concerts, Clubs, Variety, Radio and Televison.

PERSONAL MANAGER, VICTOR SEAFORTH
33 Norbury Crescent, Norbury, London SW16 4JS

DAVE SHEYRIFF

This unique act takes the 'One Man Band' to perfection catering for all tastes of musical entertainment. A wide selection of numbers in the country & pop style incorporating Guitar, Bass Drum, 'Tambouraca', Harmonica with featured lip whistling, add up to a blend of music suitable for performances at any venue.

Available for club and cabaret work Christmas 1973/74, a few dates still available in 1973.

Sole Management: JEAN M. MORLEY MANAGEMENTS
4 WOODCOTE ROAD, CAVERSHAM, READING, BERKS.

PRESENTING

*Raymond & Hilary

A MAGICAL CABARET ACT FEATURING

STAGE ILLUSIONS

ALSO **A REAL LIVE MAGICAL SHOW FOR CHILDREN**

INCLUDING LIVE DOVES & RABBITS

ENQUIRIES: 26 QUEENS ROAD MINEHEAD SOMERSET

ROY VAN DYKE

THE MAGICAL COMEDIAN

Unusual Magic - Funny Gags
- but above all it's
ENTERTAINMENT
all the way

ALSO

ROY VAN DYKE

and the

MERRY MIDGETS

A unique presentation of unusual
laugh-packed entertainment

Theatres, Clubs, TV, Cruising
Advertising, O.T.M.H., Dinners

Sole Representation & Personal Management:
John Miles, JOHN MILES ORGANISATION,
Cadbury Camp Lane, Clapton-in-Gordano,

THE INCREDIBLE SOUNDS LIKE

TONY "SHADES" VALENCE

NATIONAL DJ

Star of RADIO, THEATRE & CABARET
BBC RADIO MEDWAY
Awarded SILVER DISC for top presentation of
PHILADELPHIA SOUNDS by CBS Records

Recent successful national tours of AMERICAN BASES, MAJOR VENUES
OPEN AIR CONCERTS and support to INTERNATIONAL SINGING STARS
WHOLE SHOW comes complete with CABARET DANCERS
and LIGHTING TECHNIQUE ENGINEERS

Sole management & agency: AMEGA PROMOTIONS
468 Rochester Road, Burham, Kent.

ROY TILLEY

Entertainer Extraordinaire

COMEDY - SAX - TRUMPET - VOCAL - TAP

Enquiries: 48 Spencefield Lane, Leicester

ƒRANk TERENZI

Vocalist

RECORDING ARTISTE TV and Radio

This highly professional and versatile singer has the wonderful gift of presenting his voice with great freshness and vitality. His appeal is to the young at heart of all ages and particularly (with his dynamic looks) to the ladies. Audiences and bookers have been more than satisfied with his consistently polished performances. Frank is an entertainer in the true sense of the word and has one of the finest voices yet to break on the showbiz scene. He is also a guitarist of considerable talent.

His recent appearance on **New Faces** was proved a great success by the excellent comments from the panel, and by the work that followed.

(He is 6ft. 1 inch tall with black hair and dark eyes.)

HUTCHINSON INTERNATIONAL	NO SOLE AGENT DAVID BENNETT MANAGEMENT	PETER GROVES

NOBODY DOES IT LIKE...

LEE STEVENS

BRITAIN'S LEADING IMPERSONATOR - ENTERTAINER

RECENT BOOKINGS:

**LONDON
PALLADIUM 1974
BBC TV
"YOU ON YOUR OWN"
1975
SWEDISH TV
"CABARET" 1975
RETURN BOOKINGS ON
ALL
MAJOR BRITISH CLUBS
O.T.M.H.
VARIETY THEATRES
3 SEASONS, SOUTH
OF FRANCE**

WHAT THE PRESS SAYS

"A Solid Single"
"Professionalism all too rarely seen these days"
"Superb impression of Sophie Tucker"
"Stole first half honours at the London Palladium
with unique act, of talent, personality & professionalism"
"While there are performers like
Danny La Rue & Lee we have nothing to worry about"

P.A.: 11H Stuart Tower, Maida Vale London W9 1UH

Seen on Major Theatres and Worldwide TV
...now SOLO, presenting his new
SPECTACULAR MUSICAL ACT

JIMMY SMITH

PIANO ★ XYLOPHONE ★ HAMMOND ORGAN

Latest LP: "Loving Each Other" Ad Rhythm ARPS 4006

Enquiries for:
Theatre
Television
Radio   TO:
Clubs
Cabaret

Harold Landey,
Melton Productions
10 Cromwell Place
London SW7 2JN

SANDERS and READ

DOUBLE ACT that's good for a laugh

What's funnier than Comedy Impression?

SANDERS AND READ have a never-ending list of characters that will
make you laugh like never before.

NO SOLE AGENT

Enquiries:
74 Noakes Avenue, Great Baddow, Chelmsford, Essex.

THE SANDOWS
FIRST CLASS INTERNATIONAL
Roller Balancing Speciality

For
CABARET
*
FUNCTIONS
*
THEATRE
*
PANTOMIME
*

What the press said... ''*The Sandows got them tense again with a balancing act which, with wine glasses as a base, looked destined for catastrophe at least! It was great stuff*''.

Engagements have included Top Cabarets, Warners, Butlins, Summer Shows, Television.

Also for Children's Parties * Carnivals * Galas * Fetes.
Sandows Children's Circus
One Hour's Entertainment
Three Specialities PLUS
Stilt Walking, RUFF the Wonder Dog, TOMATO the Clown
And Audience Participation. Circus ring fence and music provided
Also Guest Artistes for larger functions. Book now for Christmas and 1976.
We claim to be the only circus that really caters for children using the art of clown comedy, and, at the same time, provides first class entertainment for parents. Our show has appeared at leading holiday centres - Butlins, Pontins (1973).
Brochure, photos: 19 College Drive, Bebington, Merseyside L63 7LN

SAVEEN

**Internationally Famous
Ventriloquist**

SAVEEN with MICKI and MACAW

RECENT SUCCESSES - ITV, BBC Television,
SAVOY HOTEL, LONDON with MICKI (the Live Talking Dog)
DAISY MAY and many other Characters.

BOOK NOW for your next Cabaret, Concert or Variety

TERRY SEABROOKE

Comedy Magical Entertainer

The comedy act that gets your audience going…
to where, it is not known!!!

BBC TV Series, Summer 1975:
"FOR MY NEXT TRICK"

All Enquiries: MELTON MANAGEMENT
10 Cromwell Place, London SW7 2JN

VICTOR SEAFORTH

COMEDIAN, IMPRESSIONIST, VOCALIST & COMPERE

VICTOR SEAFORTH has completed over 300 broadcasts and twenty-one television transmissions to date, including THE BLACK & WHITE MINSTRELS television show. He has played all the leading theatres throughout the Country, also all the top night clubs. Other credits include ten summer seasons, four pantomimes, hundreds of one night concerts and cabarets and commercial television.

Enquiries direct to VICTOR SEAFORTH
33 NORBURY CRESCENT, NORBURY, LONDON SW16 4JS

SIGHT 'N' SOUND

SIGHT 'N' SOUND are a four-piece group, specialising in vocal harmony and comedy. Experienced, professional, and ideally suitable for first class Cabaret, Cruises, Radio and Television.

AGENCY REPRESENTATION:
Malcolm Feld,
MAM Agency,
MAM House, 24/25 New Bond St.,
London W.1.

MANAGEMENT:
Mike Carroll Entertainments
42 Burford Park Road, Kings Norton,
Birmingham. B38 8PB

Simmons Brothers
COMEDY ENTERTAINERS

"HAVE A FISH!"

Summer Seasons:
'66-'67: Isle of Wight
'68: North Wales
'69: Clacton
'70: South Wales
'71: Blackpool
'72: Devon
'73: Isle of Wight
'74: Jersey
'75: Skegness

Pantomimes:
'68-'69: Bath
'70: Swansea
'71-'72: Bath
'74: Gravesend
'75: Kirkcaldy
PLUS
Thames TV: "Seeing and Doing"
Cruising for P. & O.
Extensive Cabaret Dates

All Comms: 69 St. Albans Road, Dartford, Kent DA1 1TY

THE SOUND OF
ANGELO

CLUBLAND'S FOREMOST INSTRUMENTALIST
with melodies from
Italy Spain Russia Greece

A continental artiste
Original, colourful, exciting

CABARET - CONCERT - THEATRE

All leading agencies
North - South - East - West

P.A. 6 Elton Road,
Bishopston, Bristol 7

ANGELO - THE HALLMARK OF A PROFESSIONAL

Lori Wells & The Brothers

Dynamic international cabaret entertainers.

Major cabaret venues in UK, South Africa, Australia, Israel, Malta, Bermuda,
QE2 (5 Cruises)

Sole Representation: ACTION ENTERPRISES
Suite Six, The Textile Hall, Aldams Road, Dewsbury, West Yorkshire WF12 8AE

David and Tony Webb

IDENTICAL TWINS who sing and entertain very well
Re-booked instantly at every venue they have played.

Worldwide Representation:
Michael P. Cohen,
Artists & Management.
National House, 60/66 Wardour St., London W1V 3HP

DOROTHY WAYNE

NAT BERLIN
LONDON MANAGEMENT

TED WADLEY

THE SOPHISTICATED VOCAL STYLIST
Available in England and abroad for
CABARET - RADIO - TV - FILMS
RECORDS - COMMERCIALS - CRUISING
Also available for Fashion and Advertising photography

LATEST MINI-ALBUMS INCLUDE   *"MEMORIES IN THE WATER"* CRM 50001
"THE HARVEST IS IN" CRM 50002

PA: Barnoon End , St. Ives, Cornwall TR26 1JD

Michael Vine & Karen

A strong COMEDY PATTER ACT

with the speciality of

GLAMOUR, JUGGLING and MAGIC
and hilarious Audience Participation

Suitable for CABARET or THEATRE

Enquiries: 43 Cunliffe Road, Blackpool, Lancs.

FRANK TERENZI

Summer Season '78 — Watersplash, Jersey

NEWSPAPER QUOTES: *"All in all he is quite superb".*

"He deserves network spots on T.V. Frank Terenzi whose powerful voice makes so many hit parade singers seem insipid".

"Frank is a true professional in his voice and appearance, and looks a cross between a slim Humperdinck and the Fonz".

"The star of the show singer Frank Terenzi whose interpretation of 'Breaking Up is Hard to Do' was a gem, as was Streisand's 'Evergreen'."

All enquiries to: KENNETH EARLE,
214 Brixton Road, Brixton, London SW9 6AP

THE SIMMONS BROTHERS

**The
Simmons
Brothers**

Hilarious Comedy Duo

Peter Brightman
Entertainments
Foxglove House
166 Piccadilly
London W1V 9DE

ANNE SHELTON

DAVID REID
50 London Road
London, SE23 3HF

BRIAN ROSSI

OUTSTANDING COMEDY ENTERTAINER

*Incredible success during 1978 Summer Season
at El Rancho, Jersey.*

  Sole Management: B.D.A. LIMITED
Turnpike House
31 Market Street, Leigh, Manchester

THE RITZ

SUPERB FULLY SELF CONTAINED
VOCAL HARMONY SHOW

Complete with original and very special effects this three-boy
and one-girl group are tremendously entertaining, well dressed
and have a presentation that is matchless.

(We even give you full colour posters with contracts)

Sole Representation: **Tony Sherwood**
Tony Sherwood Organisation Ltd
69B Upper Parliament Street
Nottingham NG1 6LD.

Television's International Mr Pickpocket

MARK RAFFLES

Thanks to Pierre Vickers for the Spring 1978 nationwide concert tour with the New Seekers.

Just completed work on the remake of "The Corn is Green" (starring Katharine Hepburn, directed by George Cukor) as consultant, adviser on Pickpocket sequences.

"Television's International Pickpocket" Mark Raffles certainly stole the show.

With his nimble fingers and amazing illusions he was slick, polished and totally professional. His endearing personality made him the firm favourite."
Gazette (30th June 1978)

1978 summer season Topping in the Record Breaking Show with his pickpocketing — magic and comedy at the Queen's Hall Winter Gardens, Margate.

ENQUIRIES FOR SUMMER 1979
NOW BOOKING ALL VENUES FOR THE WINTER SEASON 1978-79

Direct to P.A.: Wingfield House, Arthur Road, Cliftonville, Kent.

"The Birdman"
- Tony Durant

The BEST BIRDMAN in the BUSINESS

AUTHENTIC BIRD SOUNDS -
recognised by the Royal Society for the Protection of Birds

BIRD, ANIMAL & SOUND IMPRESSIONIST SUPREME!
–SOUND EFFECTS MAN EXTRA – ORDINARY!

Tony has appeared on Radio, T.V., Films, Theatre & Cabaret etc.

All enquiries to:
T.E.N.K. ENTERTAINMENTS
5 Triangle House, The Triangle
Clevedon, Avon

Personal Manager:
MISS POLLY PINKERTON
102 Lower Oldfield Park
Bath

DAVID NOBEL

"A smooth Bruce Forsyth that the ladies love to love and the males can't help but admire.
The smoothie with a razor wit and velvet voice"

OBSERVER 1975

Amen Ra Enterprises Ltd.
25 Jeffreys Road, London SW4

TONY JAMES
COMEDIAN / COMPERE

TONY JAMES is one of the South's up and coming young comedians. His act lasts approximately 30 to 45 minutes and can be broken into two parts

1. Dressed as a policeman (God save our Police Force!)

2. In normal evening wear, the climax being the removal of his hair piece — which is quite hair-raising!

Tony is a very clean cut comedian, with clean material.

In the past eighteen months Tony has worked with many well-known acts such as Lenny Bennett, Roger DeCourcy, The Dallas Boys, Freddie and the Dreamers, Frank Ifield, Burt Weedon, The Searchers, Charlie Williams plus many more.

**DIRECT:
TONY JAMES, 6 BLADON CLOSE, DENVILLES,
HAVANT, HANTS.**

Dick Pleasant

COMEDIAN

Member of Equity   *Several T.V. appearances*

No sole agent
P.A: 47 Gratton Court, Hartington,
Staveley, Chesterfield, Derbyshire

Robophone Answering Service if not immediately available

INTERNATIONAL COMEDY ENTERTAINER
KENNY CANTOR

PHOTO: SIR HARRY SECOMBE

**KENNY CANTOR IS FUNNY ALL OVER THE WORLD —
A TRULY INTERNATIONAL COMEDY ENTERTAINER.**

*We hope that you will enjoy seeing this musical, singing, dancing, juggling,
ad-libbing idiot, who can write, produce, design and direct his own shows.*

And just in case this isn't enough, he also appears on
Television and radio and is a recording artiste as well.

REPRESENTED BY

Jimmy Grafton Management,
10, Lesley Court,
23-33 Strutton Ground, London SW1.

Personal address:
"Ate" Pierrepont Avenue,
Gedling, Nottingham NG4 3NG.

CHRIS CHAPMAN

"MOST PLEASANT"

The Complete Entertainment Manager — Compere

Currently CRUISE DIRECTOR of the elegant "ISLAND PRINCESS"
P & O Princess Cruises — Los Angeles

Suite 520, 1850 North Whitley Ave.
Hollywood, California 90028, USA

PRINCESS CRUISES
2029 Century Park East
Los Angeles, California 90067

CHRIS BYLETT & 'DESMOND'

Featuring one of the smallest 'dolls' in the business
and perhaps the only voice of its kind used by a vent.

Personal Management: WALLY DENT

Wally Dent Entertainments
121A Woodlands Avenue
West Byfleet, Surrey.

TONY PEERS

COMEDIAN

Sole Agency:
REEVES & LAMPORT LTD.,
3, Odeon Parade,
High Street, Uxbridge, Mddx.

Mr. TERRY LANE
A Show within an Act

Terry is one of Britain's most spectacular *Comedy Female Impersonators* and with his company is the one and only spectacular star *Illusionist* in Britain today if not the world, having appeared in many leading clubs both in Britain and abroad. A very versatile act with a strong accent on comedy, both live and mime; plus a knock-out illusionist finale.
Available for: 1979 SUMMER SEASON; CABARET; ONE NIGHT STANDS; HENS; STAG NIGHTS; DAME PANTO: Season 78/79 also film, television and stage work.

Available dates rapidly disappearing.

KEITH MANIFOLD

Country-Western Vocal Guitarist
Yodelling, Monologues, Compere

OP. Knocks 1974. OP Knocks Songwriters 1976 (Singer of winning song).
Winner solo section Wembley Country Music Festival 1974. Appeared 1977
Wembley Festival.

**Available Sole or with full backing band for Tours & Cabaret at home and
abroad.**

No Sole Representation.
Les Manifold
Cornubia, Warren Carr
Matlock Derbys DE4 2LN

INTERNATIONAL DISC JOCKEY AND COMPERE

Available for cruises, radio, hotel, night club, disco's, tours, restaurants, cabaret.

(Without equipment or with my own)

My own equipment consists of stereo unit of high quality with my own radio mic, ideal for compering competitions and large light and effects road show.

Successes:

3 Summer Seasons for Butlins Holiday Centres.
"Downtown" night spot, Trondheim, Norway.
Also appeared at hotels like Inn on the Park, Park Lane, London
and many more.
NO VENUE TOO SMALL OR TOO LARGE

One of the largest Road Shows on the South Coast.

Judge Manor D.J. Promotions,
"Judge Manor", 51 The Gardens, Southwick, Brighton BN4 4AP, Sussex

UNCLE MAC PRESENTS...

AUNTY PHIL

and Her Little People
first class **UNUSUAL** *Presentation*

FAMILY "PLAY" - TIME SHOW

COMEDY ★ SINGING ★ MAGIC ★
BALANCING ★ COMPETITIONS ★ FAST MOVING
— INTEREST COMPELLING — AUDIENCE
'GET-TOGETHER' SHOW ★

Under complete control of
UNCLE MAC OUTSIDE THE BOOTH

30 to 90 mins ... Separate Adult Magic Spot
if required ... Success everywhere ...

Festivals — Fairs — Galas — Private events — Matinees — and
Corporations... Follow any act and at a reasonable fee. Offers invited for '77
Season...

Contact: 252 Oxbridge Lane,
Stockton-on-Tees,

LOVELACE WATKINS

Manager:
CHARLES O. MATHER,
International Artists
Management,
2800 Cowan Circle,
Las Vegas,
Nevada, 89107, U.S.A.

Agency Representation:
BILLY MARSH,
London Management,
235 Regent Street,
LONDON W1A 2JT

Public Relations:
CLIFFORD ELSON,
113/117 Wardour Street,
LONDON W1V 3TD

COMEDIAN, COMPERE, AFTER-DINNER SPEAKER, ACTOR, WRITER

Peter Robinson

"ALMOST TOO HUMOROUS TO MENTION"
(But still the second best comic in the business!)

Recent successes include:
"It's Cliff and Friends" for B.B.C. Television;
Congress Theatre Eastbourne; Cesar's Palace Luton;
Nottingham's Commodore; Manchester's Golden Garter;
Wakefield Theatre Club (record holder with 57 appearances!)
Leading hotels throughout the U.K.
TEN TOURS FOR COMBINED SERVICES ENTERTAINMENT
CLEAN AND CLEVER COMEDY FOR EVERY OCCASION. NOT SOLELY REPRESENTED.
TELEVISION AND RADIO SCRIPTS - PUBLICITY

P.A.: "The Chestnuts", 42 Coronation Avenue, Grappenhall, Warrington WA4 2QW

SABOTAGE

POP HARMONY CABARET GROUP
They have worked QE II, Maison Royle — Bournemouth, Winston's
— Bournemouth, Pontins — Pakefield. Ideal for clubs, bases and
cabaret venues.

MARTIN-CASSON INTERNATIONAL Entertainments Agency,
15 Silchester Road, St. Leonards-on-Sea, Sussex

ASHGAR
THE GLOBE TROTTING HYPNOTIST

Each act of Hypnotic suggestion or post Hypnotic ritual remains with the subject and spectators alike as a revelation of the possibilities inherent in man's mind and obtainable through his will.

Ashgar Productions   **Media Team Corporation**

ABBE and J.J.

PERSONALITY SONG STYLISTS
IN
VOCAL HARMONY

Brochures on Request
No Sole Representation
4 Voltaire
Ennerdale Road
Kew Gardens
Surrey TW9 3PQ

Kay Wilson & Barry Lester

Dynamic VOCAL/COMEDY/INSTRUMENTAL

Quotes from "The Stage"

Kay & Barry know exactly what to include as show stopping numbers
in a wide ranging repertoire...

Tommy Kane

I caught their act at Barnsley last week - this was a happy-go-lucky affair in which Kay made her
way around the audience dispersing the party spirit - Barry shone on guitar with his version of
Lara's Theme showing good stage sense and a flair for production technique...

James Towler

Kay & Barry brought the house down with dynamic vocal work - I predict this couple will take
the South by storm - Barry's instrumentals were gems...

Jimmy Hodges.

No sole representation. All enquiries: 183 Greensward Lane, Hockley, Essex.

WHITE GOLD

CABARET GROUP

JOHNSON & FOX ENTERTAINMENT AGENCY
52 Bewsey Street, Warrington WA2 7JE

JON MARSHALL
THE MAN WITH X-RAY EYES
presents the amazing BLINDFOLD DRIVE
a sensational outdoor attraction.

Guaranteed to keep the crowds on the edge of their seats with excitement.
Jon Marshall provides a thrilling display of driving skill after his eyes have been
sealed and hooded.

£500 Challenge

"........the EYE SURGEON who bandaged his eyes said, 'It is perfectly true
that there was no fooling, no devices, nothing. It was a fact that he did this
COMPLETELY BLINDFOLDED and with no external aid. The whole thing
was PERFECTLY THRILLING and very FASCINATING. I think it's the most
ORIGINAL stunt I have seen for many years both here and in America."

"WORLDS FAIR."

Full publicity details supplied.   All communications to:-

Bernard Woolley
    37 Regent Road
    Lostock
      Bolton, Lancs.

Telegrams Woolley 'Showbiz' Bolton Lancs.
         or
290 Oxford Gardens Stafford

BOBBY KNUTT

Management & Agency:
JOHNNIE PELLER ENTERPRISES LTD.
Saxone House, 4/8 George St., Sheffield S1 2PF

JASPER

Probably one of the fastest rising young groups around because of sheer talent. They have already topped at Bailey Clubs, Fiesta, Bunny's Place, etc and repeatedly appeared in '76 in Germany, Holland, Switzerland and Scandinavia in Cabaret and for dancing.

REPRESENTATION:

PETER McLEOD
McLeod Holden Enterprises Ltd.,
PO Box 3, Hessle, Nth Humberside

RICHARD & LARA JARMAIN

LAVISHLY COSTUMED — VISUALLY EXCITING

AN
INTERNATIONAL ILLUSION
SPECTACULAR

Recent successes include:
Greece — Portugal — Italy — Newfoundland —
Germany — Central America — Canary Isles —
Middle East — and all leading British Nightclubs, Theatres and Television.
......one of the most sought after acts in show business today.

Jan Harding

COMEDIAN

"Sorry To Bother You"

TV, FILMS, RADIO, CABARET, THEATRE,
SUMMER SEASON, PANTO, AFTER DINNER SPEAKING ETC.

49 The Chase
Clapham Common, London S.W.4.

NO SOLE AGENT

THE HARLEQUEENS

Good clean comedy mime act together with the impersonation and glamour of the top stars. Suitable for Variety Shows, Hen Nights and Pantomime

Book Direct
or
John Edward Agency, 21 Beaumont Court, Clapton, London E5 8BG

PIP & GEOFF GEORGE

A charming but punchy Vocal/Instrumental double act utilising string synthesizer/organ with full orchestral sounds — Invariably rebooked.

Summer '76 — South Pier, Blackpool.

Enquiries always welcome for cruises, cabaret, seasons, etc.

REPRESENTATION:

Peter McLeod/Roger Bloom
McLeod Holden Enterprises Ltd
PO Box 3, Hessle, Nth Humberside,

"COMEDYWISE"
COLIN GAYE

Panto 1976/77 Blackburn "Good Robber"

Nelson Firth's "Babes in the Wood"

Press - Summer:-
Colin Gaye is the ideal principal comedian. He radiates good humour and smiles his way through lively and up to date material.
"The Stage"

Press - Panto:-
Ably supporting Max Wall in second major role as Billy Goose is Colin Gaye, he had the audience in his pocket, they yelled for him, cheered him, talked back to him and loved every minute he was on stage. *"Stockport Express"*

SUMMER SEASON — PANTOMIME — SUNDAY CONCERTS —
COMEDY PLAYS — CABARET — RADIO —TV — COMMERCIALS

Enquiries: Wistonia, 152 Fairfield Road,
Morecambe & Heysham, Lancs. LA3 1LR

JUDY & CHICO

under the direction of

PETER GARRETT

Incredible
Alsatian/Yorkshire Terrier
Double Act featuring a full
programme of hilarious stunts,
which the participants obviously
enjoy as much as their audiences.

JUDY TAKES 'BABY' CHICO
OUT IN THE PRAM . . . AND SEES HIM SAFELY ACROSS THE ZEBRA.

Ideal for TV Commercials, Theatre, Outdoor Galas, etc.

Contact Direct: Peter Garrett
525 Bellhouse Road, Lower Shiregreen, Sheffield S5 0ER.

INNES ANDREWS

INTERNATIONAL CABARET ARTISTE

Clubs * Theatres * Radio * Parks * Cabaret

Enquiries to: "HEATHER HOUSE"
332 PADIHAM ROAD, BURNLEY, LANCS.

Germany * Italy * Malta * Britain

BUNNY LEWIS

STAGE AWARD WINNER '73 — Best Speciality Act.
Bill stopper on all leading cabaret bills.
A guaranteed money spinner and theatre packer.

Bunny is Box Office

TV appearances all channels.
Current film now on general release
"A Couple of Beauties".

Enquiries for first class dates only
To: MIKE PARKER
BUNNY LEWIS ENTERPRISES LTD,
41, ALEXANDRA RD SOUTH,
WHALLEY RANGE, MANCHESTER 16.
Southern Representive: Peter Elliott

CHUBBY OATES

FAT AND FUNNY

P.A: 16 CRYSTAL COURT, COLLEGE ROAD, LONDON
SE19.

DES OWEN

An experienced entertainer whose act is composed of Comedy, with
an excellent presentation of Song and Dance.
A very experienced Compere with strong personality. So successful
in 1972 season at the Summerland Entertainment Centre, Isle of
Man, has been rebooked to Star in and also to Produce his own
shows in the Summerland Showbar, 1973 season.

All Enquiries to:
191 DEVONSHIRE ROAD, BLACKPOOL FY3 7AA

Comedian, Compere, After-dinner Speaker, Actor, Writer.

PETER ROBINSON

"ALMOST TOO HUMOROUS TO MENTION"
Cabaret, Dinners, Clubs, Theatre, Summer Show,
Pantomime, Radio, Television (parts & commercials)
THEATRE dates include: Blackpool Opera House, Eastbourne Congress,
Liverpool Empire, Manchester Opera House.
HOTEL engagements include: London — Cumberland, Europa, Russell, Savoy;
Blackpool — Imperial, Savoy; Coleshill — Belfry; Manchester — Excelsior, Grand,
Midland, Piccadilly; Nottingham — Albany, Strathdon; Torquay — Imperial, etc.
CLUBS: Cresta Solihull, Golden Garter Manchester, La Strada Sunderland,
Wakefield Theatre Club, etc., etc.
OVERSEAS engagements: Gibraltar, Malta, Spain; C.S.E. tours: Singapore,
Malaya, Thailand, Libya, Cyprus, Bahrain and Persian Gulf.
"Indeed, the comedian for every occasion"
P.A. "The Chestnuts", 42, Coronation Avenue, Grappenhall,
Warrington WA4 2QW.

Johnny Cleveland

COMEDY, MUSICAL & VOCAL SPECIALITY

Personal Manager: CHIC APPLIN

STEVE COLLINS

THE YODELLING COMEDIAN

GUITAR—BANJO—VOCALS

All Enquiries: A.T.S.
City Varieties
Leeds.

SHAG CONNOR'S
CARROT CRUNCHERS

COUNTRY COMEDY MUSICAL ACT

Featuring the only known 'Beer-Drinking' Cockerel.

T.V. SHOWS TO DATE INCLUDE: WHEELTAPPERS & SHUNTERS
DAVID NIXON SHOW, SOOTY SHOW, OPPORTUNITY KNOCKS.
RECORDS AVAILABLE ON PYE (GOLDEN GUINEA)
and EMI (STARLINE)

FANTASTICALLY FUNNY ACT

SOLE MANAGEMENT AND AGENCY

Unicorn Entertainment Consultants Ltd.,
Horton Hall, Horton, Chipping Sodbury
Bristol.

DEE

STRIPTEASE SPECIALITY

All Comms:

Felicity Jane

(INTERNATIONAL SINGER)

**ACTRESS
BRITAIN'S LEADING
PRINCIPAL BOY**

**Title Roles in
Cinderella, Aladdin,
Whittington etc.
B.B.C. T.V.
O.T.M.H.**

**Appearances U.S.A.,
Australia, S. Africa**

Musicals

Revue/Feed.

Offers Invited Pantomime — Summer Season

**Personal Manager:
Harry Hollis**

**Enquiries:
1210 Carmarthen Road,
Fforestfach, Swansea, West Wales.**

PAUL FOX

PERSONAL MANAGEMENT
KENNETH EARLE

new

Sophisticated
cabaret

GAY DUO

An unusual repertoire of
original point-numbers and
tempo songs to piano
accompaniment — mostly
about the Gay way of life.
From Goblin Man and Not in
the Mood to Invitation to an
Orgy and My Guy's Gone
Straight — these numbers

provide a professional and
amusing act for Gay and
Mixed audiences alike.

A variety of spots are
available. Details from
10 Glasgow Road, Plaistow,
London E13 9HP

Brother Dominic
THE MERRY MONK OF MAGIC

**Something really different in magical entertainment
A truly international act
performed in first class mime.**

Two other non-monk acts also available.

Stage, Cabaret and all types of functions.

34 Mowbray Avenue, Blackburn, Lancs BB2 3ET

Annie Bright

SINGER 'The 99% Girl'

National Press Headlines after phenomenal success on ATV's 'New Faces':
'Dazzling' — Weekly News. 'Vocal Magic' — News of the World.
'Happy, enjoyable, sexy' — The Sun. 'A nice person with a first-class act'
—The Stage.

Now topping the bill in variety and cabaret and several TV shows (here and
abroad) lined up for 1978-79.

Representation:
Al Heath International
Global House, 9 Vastern Road, Reading RG1 8DJ.

JOHNNY CLAMP
COMEDIAN

'a gag on any subject'

VOCALIST COMPERE GUITARIST ACTOR

A VERY FAST and FUNNY COMEDIAN who is constantly employed at Night Clubs, Theatres and on Luxury Liners in all parts of the world.

He has worked with numerous stars including DIANA DORS, LULU, DICK EMERY, MORECAMBE & WISE and MOIRA ANDERSON. He has acted in Doctor Who and appeared on other TV shows and commercials.

He has a fine singing voice and like all top comics can get laughs by pulling faces. He specialises in asking the audience to choose a subject, he then tells a gag on the chosen subject.

He is dedicated to comedy and his ambition is to have his own TV series.

Enquiries:
Flat 3, 2 Wentworth Road, London N.W.11

DELAVAR
HYPNOTIST

103 ASHBY ROAD
Loughborough
Leicestershire LE11 3AB

DIRECT OR ANY REPUTABLE AGENT
24 Hour Answer Machine
Conveniently situated in centre of UK, close to East Midlands airport, handy for home or overseas flights.

JOHNNY ELK

Johnny's Herculean physique and voice to match, along with true professional magnetism will leave you with an out of this world feeling from Johnny Elk's rare talent.

He has played countless numbers of one night concerts and cabarets throughout the British Isles.

Available for one night stands, full weeks and seasons. Johnny sings ballads, country and western and rock with his own p.a. Needs no extra backing.

All enquiries to:
John Bedford Enterprises,
43 Fifth Street, Portsmouth PO1 5NA.

FINN & JONES

HILARIOUS COMEDY DUO

Appearing 78/79 Panto. Top of the Bill as The Robbers in Babes in The Wood at the Argosy Theatre, Whitehaven.

SOLE REP:

B-O-A LIMITED

Turnpike House,
31 Market Street,
Leigh, Manchester.

Rusty Goffe

4'2" INTERNATIONAL
ENTERTAINER

Featuring COMEDY, VOICE and the Greatest Smallest Sound Ever

No sole agent
Personal Manager: Leslie Collins
25 WOODBOURNE AVENUE, LONDON SW16 1UP

PAUL JAMES

"Is a very funny man"

Representation
AJAX ENTERTAINMENTS
52 Bounces Road,
London N9 8HX

LIPS

GLAMOROUS & MODERN VOCAL DUO ACT
Exceptional Vocals and Choreography

TV SHOWS:
"OPPORTUNITY KNOCKS" — "ANDY WILLIAMS SHOW"
"GET IT TOGETHER" — "STARBURST"

Worked all Major Venues throughout Europe,
Africa and the Far East.

PERSONAL MANAGEMENT & ALL ENQUIRIES:
ALAN WHITEHEAD & ASSOCIATES LTD
4 ELGIN MEWS SOUTH
LONDON W9 1JZ

JAIME ADAMS

IS FUNNY O.K.

CLUBS & HOTELS
NEW CRESTA
TALK OF THE NORTH
WALTON HALL
CLYRO COURT
CREST MOTELS
MANCHESTER CITY
ROUNDABOUT
WILLOWS
SHREWSBURY PRISON

THEATRES
ARTS
COLISEUM
THAMESIDE
NEW THEATRE
ASTORIA
PLAYHOUSE
DAVENPORT
PRESTON GUILDHALL
ALBERT HALL (BOLTON)

TELEVISION
NEW FACES
TISWAS
GANGSTERS
A.T.V.
B.B.C.
BORDER
HARLECH
SOUTHERN

"SHE'S A CRACKER" (keep her by your bread bin)

MANAGEMENT

Enquiries to:

**Bernie Lewis
Kama Management
Callaughton
Much Wenlock,
Salop TF13 6PT**

TWOGETHERNESS

Twogetherness joined together two years ago after many successes as two solo artistes. They have several summer shows and panto successes to their credit and will be available from January 1979 onwards. They have appeared in cabaret from Cornwall to Scotland.

Personal Manager:
**Mr Roy Siddons,
3 Bronte Avenue,
Bury, Lancs.**

VIC TEMPLAR

INTERNATIONAL
UNICYCLING COMEDIAN

A Riot of Laughter

Suitable for
ANY type of Entertainment

With the Great Laughter-making Audience-participation

The Miniature Cycling Competition

61 BRIXHAM CRESCENT, RUISLIP MANOR, MIDDLESEX

SHEBA

INTERNATIONAL

BELLY,

TASSEL

AND

SNAKE DANCER

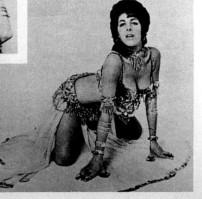

LESLIE MELVILLE

"A Bird's Best Friend"

LESLIE MELVILLE — who features MADAME CHARMAINE, The World's Greatest Clairvoyant Hen — presents a fast moving COMEDY & MYSTERY act playing for ASTONISHMENT and LAUGHS.
He gets plenty of both!!
Not 'COD' but definitely Tongue in 'BEAK!'
Cabaret successes include: Batley Variety Club, Sheffield & Stockton Fiestas, Wakefield Theatre Club, Talk of the Midlands, Wookey Hollow, Cresta Solihull etc. etc.
Summer Season 1972: Pontin's Northern Revue

NO SOLE AGENT. 104 HARROWSIDE, BLACKPOOL

WAL MAYNE AND WENDY

CHILDREN'S ENTERTAINERS

Comedy, Magic, Ventriloquism, Puppets (3 acts), Punch and Judy, Clowning, Juggling, Balloon Modelling, Music, Competitions.

Stage Show and Party Time

Entertainment with variety in entertainment

Available for: Stage, TV, Cruising, Holiday Camps, Hotels, and all private functions.

8 WETHERBY ROAD, BOREHAMWOOD, HERTS.

INCREDIBLE CHRISTOPHER

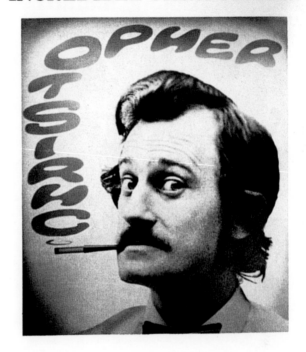

Today's Fastest (strong) COMEDY Magic Act

Several programmes

Available full weeks, weekends etc — anywhere, anytime

No sole representation, direct to:
"FERNWAY", FISHBOURNE LANE, ISLE OF WIGHT PO33 4EX

Roy & Jackie Toaduff

International Entertainers

Six Royal Performances
Major Theatre and Cabaret circuits on four Continents

"Professional polish of a dazzling duo"
"Britain's right royal ambassadors at large" — vide Press.

No sole agent. Personal Manager: COLIN EDWARDES
CHANTRY HOTEL, DRONFIELD, SHEFFIELD, YORKS.

CHARLIE SMITHERS

COMEDIAN

Stage Award Winner 1972

MECCA AGENCY INTERNATIONAL LTD. 22 Shaftesbury Ave,
London W1V 8AP.

ROGER SALTER
"The Natural Entertainer"

COMEDIAN

*

COMPERE

*

VOCALIST

*

OLD TYME
MUSIC HALL

*

PANTOMIME

*

ACTOR

SPECIALITIES
Comedy/Vocal Acts * Accents and Dialects * Master of Ad-Lib *
Music Hall Chairman * Pantomime Dame * Character Actor *
Original and International Material * Language Knowledge (French,
Spanish, German, Italian)

WORK SOUGHT
As above plus T.V. work, commercials, voice-overs, films,
broadcasting, scriptwriting

5 WARWICK DRIVE, UPPER RICHMOND ROAD,
LONDON SW15 6LB.

CLIVE WEBB

is definitely Barmy!

London
Palladium

Futurist
Scarbro'

Spa Royal
Bridlington

Pier Theatre
Skegness

Empire
Sunderland

Alhambra
Sheffield

Floral
Scarboro

W. Gardens
Morecambe

Caesars
Palace

Golden
Garter

Jollees

Night Out

Wakefield
Theatre Club

Stardust
Usk

Wookey
Hollow

Crystal
Rooms,
etc.

THEATRES / CLUBS / TV / RADIO / FUNERALS

**Personal Management — Peter McLeod
McLEOD HOLDEN ENT. LTD.**

A note on the author

James Innes-Smith divides his time between Central London and LA, and is extremely fond of small dogs. He is an actor and the author of *Bad Hair* and *Big Hair*.

Visit James Innes-Smith at 'The Weird and the Wonderful' website: www.theweirdandthewonderful.com for lots more silliness.

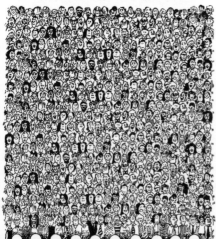